Quantum Physics: Get What You Want

Practical Quantum Physics Tips to Attract Health, Happiness, Wealth & Abundance

Copyright Maya Faro© 2016

Maya Faro © Copyright 2016-2023 - All rights reserved.
ISBN: 978-1-80095-102-0

Legal Notice:

This book is copyright protected. It for personal use only.

Disclaimer Notice:

Please note the information contained in this document is for educational and entertainment purposes only. Every attempt has been made to provide accurate, up to date and completely reliable information. No warranties of any kind are expressed or implied.

Readers acknowledge that the author is not engaging in the rendering of legal, financial, medical or professional advice. Readers agree that under no circumstances are we responsible for any losses, direct or indirect, which are incurred as a result of the use of information contained within this document, including, but not limited to, errors, omissions, or inaccuracies.

Contents

Introduction 7
Chapter 1: What is Quantum Physics? 9
Chapter 2: What Does This Have to do With Me? 21
Chapter 3: Understanding Affirmations 26
Chapter 4: Creating a Powerful Affirmation 39
Chapter 5: Reprogramming for Wealth and Success 50
Chapter 6: Reprogramming for Healthy Relationships 56
Chapter 7: Better Time Management Using Reprogramming 67
Chapter 8: See Your Stress and Anxiety Go Away 79
Chapter 9: Tips to Bring About Positive Energy 83
Conclusion 88

Introduction

Congratulations on taking an interest in *Quantum Physics to Get What You Want: Practical Quantum Physics Tips to Improve Your life, Attract Health, Happiness, and Money*, and thank you for doing so.

The following chapters will discuss some of the basics of quantum physics and how it can make a big difference in your life. Most people assume that quantum physics is too complicated and that the only application for it is in a lab, so it would never have anything to do with their lives. But in reality, quantum physics and some of the theories behind it have everything to do with the how your life is playing out.

The idea behind this theory is that your emotions and feelings send off energy through the universe. This energy will then match up with particles out there, ones that have no state. Once these energies match, the particles will activate into a state and send the same energy back to you. This is going to influence the way that your life will turn out and the types of things that come up. With positive energy, you are going to be able to get the good health, wealth, and relationships that you want.

This guidebook is going to take the time to look at how these ideas in quantum physics are going to help you to get the life that you have always dreamed about. In addition to talking about quantum physics and the basics behind it, we will take a look at how affirmations can help, how you can change the energy, and even how you can bring about the great things that you want in your life.

You hold the destiny to having health, wealth, and happiness in your life. With the help of this guidebook, you will be able to get the life that you want with the help of positive thinking!

There are plenty of books on this subject on the market, thanks again for choosing this one! Every effort was made to ensure it is full of as much useful information as possible. Please enjoy!

Chapter 1: What is Quantum Physics?

Before we get into the basics of how this type of physics can help you improve your life, let's take a look at the basics behind quantum physics and what it all entails.

If you have ever been in a science classroom, you may have heard about quantum physics and how it is a more advanced field in the science realm. Some may be happy that they just needed to take the basics of science in high school and college and that they never needed to get so high up to learn about this field of physics.

Despite the complex thoughts that go with quantum physics, it is a fascinating study and one that can improve your life when you learn the basic principles that work behind it. Let's take a look at quantum physics and get a feel for it before moving into the different ways that you can get quantum physics to work to better your life.

What is quantum physics?

So, the first question that you may have is what quantum physics is. This is the study of energy and matter at the molecular, nuclear, atomic, and even microscopic levels. It was discovered during the 20th century that the laws governing macroscopic objects would not function the same way if they were placed on a smaller level. Many scientists started working to learn the differences between how the macro and micro worked and why they were so different.

The Latin meaning for quantum is "how much." This refers to the small units of energy and matter that are first predicted by quantum physics as well as observed within this science. Even time and space have miniscule values that can be discovered in this kind of science, even though they may seem enormous at first.

Before the 20th century, scientists had made great strides in figuring out how the world worked. But they lacked the technology to be able to look at their measurements with the highest precision. They often assumed that the measurements they took on the biggest part of the object would be the same throughout the object.

But over time, they were able to gain the technology that added more precision to their measurements, and some strange things were then observed. It was during 1900s that quantum physics was born thanks to a paper by Max Planck that talked about blackbody radiation. Along with Niels Bohr, Albert Einstein, Erwin Schrödinger, and others, there was a lot of development that was done on this field over the years. The surprising part is that Einstein had some issues with the theories behind quantum physics and he tried to make modifications to and disprove the theories, even though his work was later used to make more breakthroughs in the study.

At this point, you may be wondering what is so special about quantum physics. Why do you need to learn about science to get something good to happen in your life? In the realm of quantum physics, when you observe something, you can influence the processes that are taking place physically. Light waves will act like particles, and the particles will behave like waves.

Matter can go from one spot to another without having to move through the space between the two places, a process known as quantum tunneling. Information can move across a vast distance instantly.

The unique thing that comes up with quantum mechanics is that the universe is a series of probabilities. It is going to break down when you are dealing with a large object, but the possibilities are all there, waiting to see what will happen to them next. You can have some choice in influencing them if you know how to do it.

Yes, this does sound confusing, and when you start to get into all the formulas and trying to estimate how atoms are going to work, it is something that can stretch the brain a bit. But in this book, we are not going to focus so much on the specifics of each atom and molecule. This isn't going to be a textbook. We will discuss how you can use some of these theories, and even change some aspects of your life, to allow quantum physics to work to better your life.

There are several types of quantum physics that you may work with, including the following:

Quantum entanglement

This is one of the key concepts of quantum physics, and it describes a situation where a multitude of particles are associated in such a way that measuring the quantum state of just one of these particles will also place constraints on the measurement of the others.

One of the best known examples of quantum entanglement is the Einstein-Podolsky-Rosen Paradox (or the EPR Paradox). This paradox involves two particles that are entangled together according to quantum mechanics. Each of these particles is uncertain of its state until it is measured, and once it is measured, that state will suddenly become certain. At the same time, the other particle's state is going to become certain as well. This is a paradox because it seems that the communication between these two particles happens faster than the speed of light.

This is a unique paradox. You have two particles that have no idea of what they are doing at the time. They are both in uncertain states, though they are bound together. When you measure one of them, the state becomes certain for both of them at the same time. And since the particles are considered possibilities in the world before they are measured, there are endless possibilities that both of these could turn into in the result.

So, what does this paradox mean? It means that until the moment you measure the particles, they are not going to have a definite quantum spin, but they are waiting to find out their possible states. As soon as you measure the spin of the first particle, you will know the value that you will get if you chose to measure the spin of the second particle. This is because both of the particles must equal zero, like they did in the beginning, so whatever the first particle is measured at, the second one should be the negative of it.

Quantum optics

This is another branch of quantum physics that concentrates most on the behavior of photons, or light. When working with quantum options, you will be studying how the behavior of each photon will individually have a bearing on how the light comes out. One of the applications that have been discovered using quantum optics includes lasers.

Quantum electrodynamics

This is the study of how photons and electrons interact on a micro level. It was first developed in the 1940s by Richard Feynman, Sin-Itro Tomonaga, and Julian Schwinger, among others. The predictions that came from the use of QED in regards to the scattering of electrons and photons was pretty accurate; it got to the point that it was correct up to eleven decimal places each time.

These are just some of the theories that have come out of the study of quantum physics. Many scientists have worked to understand more about this part of physics as well as trying to reconcile this theory with some of the ideas that Einstein came up with earlier on. Despite the different tests, the rules that accompany quantum physics seem to be different than what are found with other types of objects, making for a fascinating study.

Things that you should know about quantum physics

One of the reasons that quantum physics is so hard for people to understand right at the beginning is because it is counter-intuitive. Everything that you have learned in the past about atoms, molecules, and other particles seems to go out the window when you get to quantum physics. Even some of the physicists who work with it every day have some issues comprehending what is going on.

But despite all of this confusion, quantum physics does not have to be incomprehensible. There are six concepts that you should keep in mind when you are trying to learn more about quantum physics that will also help it make more sense.

1. Everything is made out of waves and particles

The first thing to understand is that everything in our universe has a wave nature and a particle nature at the same time. With the particles that are talked about in quantum physics, the wave isn't moving at all, but there is still a wave nature present that will go off once you measure that particular particle.

2. This kind of physics is considered probabilistic

This is one of the most controversial as well as surprising parts of working with quantum physics. It is almost impossible to predict with absolute certainty what the outcome of an experiment will be. When physicists try to predict the results of their experiment, the prediction is always made in the form of a probability that lists out how likely it is for finding each of the different outcomes. It often takes quite a few experiments to figure out these probabilities rather than just one.

This is controversial because it has confused people for a long time. Our modern physics likes the idea that when you perform an experiment, it is going to happen the same way each time that you do it. But this is not so with quantum physics. You could try out the experiment ten times and get a different result each time, or maybe have the same result six times and then entirely different ones for the other four times. There is no guarantee what you will get, so they are all listed as probabilities.

This is also a part of the theory that leads to the idea that a particle could be in many different states at a time. All that scientists can predict is the probability of something happening, and then when they start to do the measurements, the particle will take on a particular state based on all the possibilities that it could go to. Now, some people assume that the particle can be in all states at once until you measure it out, and others believe that the particle is in just one state that is unknown before being measured to pick the right state.

3. Quantum physics is considered non-local

This was discovered thanks to the EPR paper that argued that quantum physics would allow the existence of systems where measurements that were made at one location would be able to affect the other particle, even if they occurred at places that were far apart. This made many people believe that the outcomes of the measurement must be predetermined because it was too fast, going quicker than the speed of light, to change both particles at the same time.

While the paper tried to prove that these outcomes must be predetermined, they were not able to do this. The common approach that is used to understand these results is to say that quantum mechanics is non-local. This means that there is no way to explain how these signals get to each other when using the speed of light because they are so much faster.

Scientists are still working to figure this out. Einstein was one of the first who didn't understand how this worked, and while he tried to work with the EPR paper to prove that this part of quantum physics didn't work, he seemed just to prove that it is something that does happen. Over the years, people have tried to use this to explain wormholes and other unique things that occur in the scientific field.

If you are feeling a little bit confused by how all of this works, don't worry, you are not alone. Even scientists are confused by how these particles react in different ways than expected. The rules of quantum physics are not going to follow the rules that are set out in other branches of physics, which can make them confusing, but fascinating at the same time. Luckily, you will be able to use this information and the fact that the particles can react in different ways over time to your advantage, as we will point out in the following chapters.

Dealing with quantum physics can seem confusing, and for those who haven't worked in this field, it can be strange to think that some particles don't have states or that they are going to change instantly when just one of them are measured. But you will learn how to make these work in your favor to improve your life and personal relationships!

Chapter 2: What Does This Have to do With Me?

So far we have spent some time looking at the basics of quantum physics. There is so much more to it, but the previous chapter can help us understand how we can make things work the way that you want. So let's take another look at quantum physics and learn how you can use these basics to make the changes you want in your life.

The idea behind this is that the two particles are in either multiple states at once or an unknown state. We don't know what state they are in, and this can regularly change until you measure one of the particles. The other particle will have changed at the same time. Once the measurement is done, you will find that the state of the particles is determined.

With that in mind, the next thing to consider is how these particles are going to change. One of the unique things that happen with quantum physics is that none of the particles have to change in a certain way. Studies have been done on various particles, and each time it comes up with different answers. Keep in mind that the predictions about how a particle will respond vary based on probability, not certainty.

The new question is, what affects how the particle is going to react? In most physics, you know that if certain conditions are met and kept constant, you are going to have the same reaction happen each time. For example, when you drop a ball from the same height each time, it will bounce down on the ground at the same speed every time. But with quantum physics, these particles aren't going to work the same way as most other issues. You may keep all of the parts constant, but they will give a different result each time you do the work. This doesn't make sense in the science and physics world, but it is what happens when you are working in quantum physics.

Some believe that you can influence the ways the particles react based on your thoughts and perceptions. If you are having a bad time or are in a bad mood one day, you may find that the particles react in one way, but if you are in a good mood and think in a positive way, you will find that you can get the particles to react in a different way.

Think of what this all means. You get the power to dictate how particles are going to react, even if you aren't in the lab trying to see how they work. You don't need the big labs, fancy tools, or lots of time to practice how the particles are going to react. Instead, you can learn how to use your energy, positive thoughts, and outlook on life to change the way that the particles behave in your life, and you can bring in so much more of the good stuff that you want.

On the same line, you may also be the reason that the bad things are going on in your life. For example, if you are having trouble with money, can't keep your job, or are having trouble with relationships, it may be the way you are reacting with the particles around you. If you are focusing too much on these negative things, always in a foul mood, or have other issues that are going on that keep you from being happy and optimistic, this energy is coming from you and affecting how the particles will be measured and react to you. They can turn around and bring you more negativity based on the energies that you are sending out into the universe.

Luckily, you can make a difference in how this all works for you. You are not stuck with the bad luck, the hard time with a job, or any of the other issues that may already be plaguing your life. You just need to change the way that you react to things around you. With some positive thinking, hard work, and a good mood most of the time, you will react with the particles to get the things that you want in your life.

There are so many great things that you can do with quantum physics and making the particles react in certain ways. You can gain more money. You can finally get those great relationships that you want. You can enjoy life and become more successful than you could imagine, all because of the way that YOU are reacting with the particles that are around you.

We will show you how you can get these particles to react the way that you want. Whether you are looking to turn your bad fortunes around or you are finally ready to get out of that rut that you have been in for so long, you can definitely use quantum physics to help you out. Who would have thought that physics could really help you out with your life!

Chapter 3: Understanding Affirmations

We have taken a bit of time to talk about the basics of quantum physics and even how it relates to your daily life. Your thoughts and attitude have a lot to do with what is going to happen in your life. When you are negative or focus only on the bad things that are going on in your life, you are causing the particles around you to turn out negative. You are going to keep having these same bad things stay around in your life. It is a vicious cycle that can be almost impossible to fix, but you have the power to change your outlook on things and change how the particles react.

So basically, when you are ready to take charge of your life and really get the great stuff, wealth, success, and good relationships, it is all about how you work with these particles. Yes, there may be some things that are negative in your life, but that doesn't mean that you need to focus on them. The better thing to do is concentrate on the good things that are already in your life, or even on the things that you would like to see in your life. You have to stay positive, and that will change how the particles are reacting in your life, and you will see how these things begin to come your way.

Staying resolute is going to be the hardest part. When things get you down, you are automatically going to want to think, "Why does this always happen to me?" A better way to react would be, "Well, at least I have my family and a great job!" It will take some time to get this down because we are so used to just focusing on the negative things, but with practice, you will find that it is easier to think in a positive way and improve the quality of your life.

One of the ways that you are able to do this is to work on affirmations. Affirmations are used all around the world by people who are looking to become stronger in their belief systems or even improve their situations. They have a high rate of success thanks to the ability to use inner dialogue in a positive way. This positivity will affect your mind subconsciously and will allow you to adopt your newfound belief system; in this case, it is all about having a more positive lifestyle.

The idea behind affirmations is similar to what you will find when using quantum physics to improve your life. It recognizes that your subconscious mind has a direct influence on your actions and the way that things are going on around you. While it is difficult to control the way that the subconscious is going to work, there are ways that you can guide it and influence it, and this is where affirmations are going to come in to help you out.

You can make affirmations as simple or as complicated as you need to begin having positive thoughts to start having a positive impact on your life. Short positive statements that you either say in your head or read aloud will have a huge impact. You would be amazed at how much of a difference a few minutes of positive thoughts through affirmations can make in how you react to the world around you. Of course, if you need to spend a bit more time to help you get your mind to turn from the negative thoughts and instead focus on the positive ones, this is perfectly fine. It is just to show that you are able to get all the benefits no matter how much time you have to devote to it each day.

Over time, these positive statements are going to manifest themselves into positive thoughts and can even change the way that you perceive yourself. It may take some time, but soon you will start to notice a new and even improved you. Your conscious mind will need to start realizing that there are a lot of negative thoughts that are going through your head each day. You will be amazed at how many times you feel cynical about the things around you in a day. And when you are aware of the negative thoughts, you can slowly replace them and start using thoughts that are positive and more inspiring towards your goals.

Affirmations are not hard to start implementing into your schedule. Some of the things that you should remember when getting started with affirmations include:

- All of your affirmations need to be in the present tense. You should also focus on having already achieved whatever you desire. Focus on what it feels like to have that item or success in your life.
- The affirmation needs to be filled with positivity. Check the negativity at the door or you are going

to be influencing your particles in the wrong way. Even if the goal seems unrealistic, just keep working towards it and have a 'can-do' attitude while you are doing the affirmation.
- Each affirmation should have some meaning behind it. You need to make sure that the affirmation is able to resonate emotionally with you so that you can say them with some passion. Pick something that you really want, such as healthy relationships or success, and it will work better.

Don't worry; this isn't something that has to be overly complicated, and we will include some exercises that will help you to gain the knowledge needed to make your affirmation shine. But when you add in the principles talked about above and work to do affirmations each day, you will find that the new things that come into your life are so much better than most people can dream about. Right from the moment that you start, you are influencing how the universe reacts to you and are making sure that the particles in quantum physics come to work for your life.

Understanding how affirmations work

The main point behind affirmations is that they work to reprogram your mind. When it is done the right way, it has the power to transform so many things in your life. It makes impossible things seem possible. It improves your health, your relationships flourish, and even success will come knocking on your door.

The idea is that the human brain is similar to a computer. With years of trying to keep up with the Joneses and hearing in the media that we need more and more, it has become hard to realize that what we have is already so important and great. We are used to telling ourselves that we aren't rich enough, successful enough, or good looking enough. And these thoughts have enormous negative impacts on our life. We are feeding our minds viruses, Trojan horses, and other harmful things and still hoping to come out on top in the end. Does your computer work well when it is bogged down by viruses? No, and neither does your brain.

To make things better, you need to override the program, the negative thoughts, and instead, train them to be positive. You need to immerse yourself in this new concept of positive thinking and believing the impossible while kicking out those negative thoughts as quickly as possible.

The way that you do this is by keeping up with your affirmation. Unfortunately, you are not able to do an affirmation every once in a while and then wonder why it isn't working out the way you had hoped. You need to spend time with affirmations, at least ten or fifteen minutes each day, and do it on a consistent basis to kick those negative vibes out and bring in all the great things you want out of life.

There are many things that you can use affirmations for to reprogram how the mind will work. Some of these include:

- Strengthening your vision
- Getting healthier hair
- Creating the ideal body
- Losing weight
- Making the mind stronger
- Learning how to be more forgiving

- Attracting your soul mate
- Growing a business
- Overcoming issues with procrastination
- Overcome your fears
- Healing the disease that is slowing down your body
- Making more friends
- Having better health
- Making more money
- Buying a new home
- Becoming more attractive

The list can go on. If you want to make a change for the better in your life, you can use affirmations to help you get there. You just need to believe that these things can happen and stay consistent with your affirmations each day, and you will see the results that you want.

Now we need to look more at how affirmations are going to work in particular and then how they are going to link back to the particles that we talked about in the previous chapters.

When you are going through something in life, whether it is positive or negative, you are going to have some adamant emotions. If you are happy, this is something that others can feel and notice when they are around you. But the same can be said about anger and sadness. All of these emotions can come from you due to your personal energy.

This personal energy is going to send out strong vibrations around the body, and these vibrations will then send signals out to the world around you just like a satellite does with its frequencies. What you send out is going to be matched. Those particles that are in unknown states are going to react to those vibrations that you send out, whether they are positive or negative, and send back a match to you.

If you are sending out negative vibrations, these particles are going to react in a way that will send back more negative things to you. This is why some people seem to get in a rut and just can't seem to turn things around as more and more negative things come into their lives. The good news is that when you send out those positive vibrations, the particles around you will send back the same positive things to you, which can significantly improve your life. Both are cycles that show just how powerful our emotions can be and how much they influence our lives.

Of course, there are going to be times when bad things do occur. You aren't going to be able to use this to avoid all negative things. But the way that you react to negative occurrences in your life will make a big difference on the future events that will happen to you. Yes, losing someone you love or having trouble at work can be an issue, but this is why you should focus on the possibilities that can happen in the future.

Think about all the good things that you want to occur in the future. Reflect on that business success, that weight loss, that good relationship, or any other thing that you want to happen in the future that is good. These will get you through those hard times and can help you to get out of the rut before it even begins. The particles are going to respond to whatever vibrations you are sending out, regardless of your current situation.

If you are feeling down or like the day is just not going your way, it is time to change that mind over to something positive. This is something that you can easily do with just a few moments to yourself. Consider sitting in silence and just saying, "I feel great!" Just by saying this, you are going to train the mind to start looking for times in your past when you did feel great. This is often enough to help you to get through that difficult point by feeling better and sending out the right vibrations.

An exercise to try out

We have spent a lot of time in this chapter talking about affirmations and how they can influence the vibrations that you are sending out to the world. Now let's take some time to do an exercise to help you practice affirmations and to see how great they can be.

The first thing you will need to do to practice affirmations is to make out a list of the things that you to do and to have in the future. You can even include some of the things that you want to be in the future as well. The list doesn't have to be extremely long, but think about the things that you would like to have in the future and write them down.

As you are listing each one of these items, pay some attention to the feelings that come when you are writing. You can write these feelings down right next to the items on the list. For the most part, you are going to find that you feel inadequate because you are so far behind where you want to be.

Now, take a second and imagine that there are no obstacles in your life. You can do anything you want and achieve any goal you want because all of the barriers are gone. How does this feel? It probably feels pretty good when you imagine yourself reaching those goals.

Go through the list again so that you can put the new feelings down by each of the goals. They may seem impossible at that time, but don't worry about that. Just focus on the good feelings, the ones that you got when you imagined that anything is possible, while you are finishing the list and when you are doing the real affirmation down the line.

This is now going to become your guide when you are creating affirmations. When it is your time of day to do an affirmation, or you need a mental pick up from some hard knocks that life threw at you, you can bring out this list. Remember the good feelings that you had when you thought of all the things you could do when you got rid of all those obstacles. It may seem like a silly thing to do, but just reminding yourself of positive feelings, as well as reminding yourself of the goals that you want to do in life, can help to change your negative vibes into good ones, and that will make all the difference in the world.

Affirmations can make all the difference between changing your vibes from positive to negative. When you are sending out a vibe to the particles around you, wouldn't it be better to have positive vibes of health, luck, and happiness come back, rather than negative ones that can make life more difficult?

Chapter 4: Creating a Powerful Affirmation

By this point, we have discussed a bit more about creating affirmations and why they are so important. We have learned that the emotions we have during our lives are powerful and they can send energy out to the universe based on the feelings that we are having. This energy can meet with the particles that are discussed in quantum physics as having no state, but once they reach the particles, they are going to send similar energy back to you.

This is why, when you can send out the positive energy, being happy for the things that are already in your life or looking forward with positivity to the things that you want in your future, you are going to get more of that positive energy coming right back to you. On the other hand, the same thing can be said about the negative emotions as well. If you are dealing with a lot of negative things in your life and can't catch a break, it may be time to look at the energy that you are sending out to the world.

Creating the right affirmation for you

Now it is time to look at the process of creating affirmations in your life. You want to do this in the right way to ensure that your subconscious is being reprogrammed and to know that you are now sending out positivity. The words that you say aren't the only important part; you also need to concentrate on the way you say the words.

Think of it like this: You may hear someone say something, but if they don't have feeling behind it, and they sound like they are being forced to say the words, how likely are you to believe them? But if that same person came out with a lot of conviction and were ready just to jump up and get things done, you would probably be able to feel that positive energy from them and you will believe they will succeed.

You need to do the same thing when you are working on your affirmations. You need to have conviction, the right words, and a positive outlook to go with it all. Let's take a look at some of the things that you should add in when you are trying to create the right affirmations.

The first thing that you should do is phrase the affirmation in the way that is the most positive. Make sure that they stay focused, simple, short, and clean. Going on for an hour about the affirmation is not going to give the same ring to it, and you are going to get bored and start sending off the wrong energy. Rather, keep it to the point and dynamic in the hopes of triggering explosive feelings in your mind.

Let's take the example of someone who is trying to stop smoking. Some will make the mistake of saying something like "I don't smoke any longer. I don't need to have a cigarette. Cigarettes are unhealthy." This one isn't effective because you are not removing the desire for cigarettes at all, and since you are repeating the word cigarette multiple times in the affirmation, you are causing problems. The mind is going to keep hearing the word 'cigarette' rather than all the other words, and soon they are the focus of your affirmation, going against the whole point here.

Instead of focusing on cigarettes, you should focus on what it would mean if you could stop smoking. It may mean that you are going to feel healthier, that you can gain freedom, and that you will feel better. Your affirmations should include these aspects to keep your mind on the positive, rather than on the negative. A good statement to use would include: "I feel healthy and energetic and I'm so much happier with the healthier choices I am making!"

The affirmation also needs to have some feeling. If you are neutral about the feelings that you are getting out of the affirmation, you are doing a bit better than the negative energy, but you are still missing out on all the great things that you can get from the positive energy. Think of things to say that will create a powerful feeling that is positive.

Being whimsical and lively are great ways to go about doing this. They can help you get some of those emotions through the door and can make your mind feel excited with all that dynamic flow. The highly emotional ones are also easier for the mind to hold onto, making it simpler to keep these positive feelings going.

A good way to do this is to use affirmations on a daily basis, but you will still need to craft the affirmations the right way. You want to create an affirmation that will help you to manifest these changes you desire. The issue often comes when people confuse affirmations with some other options, such as vision boards and dream cards. While these are great ways to make the positive statements that you need, they should not be considered part of the affirmation.

To get the affirmation to work properly, you need to understand that to manifest something with your new energy, you will need to find a way to change yourself into the thing that you want. Until you are that person, you won't be able to create these lasting changes for yourself. Affirmations are not always about the things that you want; they are more about who you want to become.

Here is a little example of how this would work in the form of losing weight. Lots of people want to lose weight, but they just aren't sure how to go about it. They may have tried countless diets and exercise programs to no avail. You can use affirmations to help out with this as long as you do it in the proper way.

Instead of focusing on the dieting, you need to make yourself into a person who has already lost weight. Think about the thoughts this person will have when they have lost the weight. What beliefs do they hold; what actions do they take? Someone who has already lost weight is going to have a different set of beliefs and will go through various steps when it comes to eating and food compared to someone who is still struggling to make this happen. When you start to think like a person who has already lost weight, you can easily bring in the energy that you need while also learning the tricks that will help that stubborn weight to come off.

Creating your wealth or starting a new business is going to work in a similar way. If you want to become wealthy, you need to become someone who has already gained wealth. Someone who is wealthy has a particular set of thoughts on investing, debt, and money when compared to you who may be struggling to get by. They have certain habits and traits that you should start copying if you would like to gain more wealth.

Write down some of the traits and habits you think they have. You need to remember these traits and characteristics and start to bring them into your life. You will find that with the right positive actions and the good energy that is coming to you with these changes in perception, you too can start to have some of that great wealth you've been dreaming about.

The basic things that you need to know about creating your affirmations is that they need to be heartfelt. You need to mean them, as in you need to bring out the emotions when you are saying the affirmation. You need to focus on what you will become in the future when you reach the goal rather than focusing on all the things you are missing out on now. When you can carry these two elements together inside of your affirmations, you will find that it is easier than ever to get the right energy sent out and to make quantum physics work for you.

Affirmations to help reprogram yourself

Strong and powerful affirmations are one of the best tools that you can use to make changes to your life while reprogramming your subconscious mind. This is going to help you create some new habits, actions, and thoughts that can be more positive and will send out the good energy that you want.

There are some guidelines that you should follow if you are looking to reprogram the way that your mind is working. The first thing that you should consider is starting your affirmation using the words, "I am." These are some of the most powerful words in our language, and the mind has a way of interpreting them as a direct order to make something happen. It does not matter if the statement isn't true; the mind will start to work to make it true.

You should also say the affirmation in the present tense. You should make the affirmation powerful by describing the thing that you have in a way that tells the mind you already have it. Also, state the affirmation in a positive way. Never say in the affirmation what you don't want, because it will assume that what you are saying is what you want. Only say the things that you want to happen, and ignore the rest. For example, if you state, "I am no longer angry," your mind is just going to hear, "I am angry."

Another thing we discussed earlier that you should keep in mind is that the affirmation should be short and precise. You want it to be similar to an advertising slogan in that it is easy to remember so you can repeat it when needed. But you should also include some details in the affirmation to make it more powerful. For example, instead of just saying that you are driving a car, state what kind of car you are driving.

Action words can help out with your affirmation because they will add some more power. So make sure to get those '-ing' words into the affirmation as much as you can. Feeling and dynamic words can make a big difference as well because they will help to influence your emotions. 'Lovingly,' 'happily,' and 'enjoying' are words that are considered dynamic because they can bring out certain emotions in the mind, even if they are not true at that moment.

One last thing to do before you end your affirmation is to add "this or something better!" to the end. This helps to avoid limiting what your energy can send out. When you are done with listing out your short affirmation, make sure to say something like, "This or something better is now real for me!" You can now get rid of some of the limitations, open up your mind to more benefits, and the positive energy that is going to come off you and get sent out to the particles is going to be unreal.

Some of the affirmations that have the power that you want so that you can reprogram some of your beliefs include:

- Each day I am better!
- I am a creative and powerful being
- Everything is timed to enter into my life at the perfect moment
- Everything I want comes to me effortlessly, with great joy, and quickly
- I am successful and happy
- I feel a connection to the source that guides me to my ultimate destination in life
- I am a creative and powerful center

Keep in mind that while affirmations are powerful, they do take some time. Our modern society has made it so easy to let the negative emotions and energy in that it can be hard for the affirmations to compete. Remember that you are trying to reprogram your whole mind and that this isn't something that is going to happen for you overnight. But with some perseverance and hard work, you will find that the affirmations are going to give you the tools to get out there and see a difference.

Chapter 5: Reprogramming for Wealth and Success

One of the strongest wishes that many people have is to get wealth and success. Perhaps they are tired of always working hard and never seeing any results. They are still living paycheck to paycheck, hoping to get ahead someday. Or they may see how other people are becoming wealthy and wish to have that kind of lifestyle as well. While all of us wish to be rich, or at least have enough money to live comfortably, this is not a reality for quite a few people only because they aren't taking the right steps.

Affirmations can be an effective tool for bringing more wealth and success into your life. If you use it the right way, they will be able to make changes from the inside out. You will be able to attract the wealth that you want for your life. If you are looking to use affirmations to bring about more prosperity in your life, here are a few techniques that you can try as well as some of the things that you should avoid, so you don't bring about the wrong kind of energy in this process.

First, remember that affirmations are statements of your intent. They are going to be used to describe the reality that you want rather than the reality that you are living in now. You will need to state them in the present tense, but you are telling yourself that you can quickly bring in the money that you want, and then that energy is going to be sent back to you. For example, if you want to start earning a decent wage, you may use an affirmation such as, "I easily make six figures or more in income." This is short and sweet and to the point, but during your session of affirmation, you will repeat this statement over and over with conviction.

Some people may have been intrigued by the idea of doing affirmations in the past, gave it a try, and felt that they didn't work for them. You need to keep in mind that just stating something over and over again is not going to be enough for this to work. You need to say it with power and mean what you are saying.

One way to focus on the phrases and make them work for you is to try putting a picture behind the statements. For example, if you are trying to gain more wealth, play out a scenario in your head that imagines you as rich.

How will you feel when you don't have to worry about bills anymore? How will it feel when you can purchase the things that you need and want without feeling worried? While you are going through your statement, focus on these scenes with a fierce intention, and you will be amazed at how much more powerful your affirmations can be.

At this point, you are probably wondering what affirmations you can say to bring more wealth into your life. There are countless books and online resources that you can use that will list out different wordings of affirmations. You are more than welcome to use these, as well as a few suggestions that we will post below, but you should make sure that it resonates with you. It is hard to put intent and feeling behind an affirmation if you just randomly pick one off the page. Say one that taps into your feelings and emotions, and that you connect with, and the affirmation will be so much better. Using the affirmations in this book are a good way to get started so that you know the proper wording, but change them to work for you.

Some of the affirmations that you can use to reprogram your mind for more wealth include:

- Financial opportunities are attracted to me.
- I earn and spend my money in a wise manner
- It is my right to have wealth
- I find it easy to make money

These are good starting points to help you get your affirmations off the ground. But you should always tailor them to meet your needs. If one feels awkward to you or just doesn't connect with your emotions, just throw it out and try something new. These affirmations are supposed to strike a chord with you, to make you feel something, and you can always mix and match statements to make them your own.

Exercise

Now that you understand the basics of using affirmations to draw wealth to yourself and the benefits of being good friends with money and imagining yourself as rich, it is time to try out a few exercises to give you some practice. Once you are done with this practice, you will be able to use affirmations on a daily basis to bring in the money that you desire.

To start this exercise, go to a room where you can be alone, at least for a few minutes. Ideally, you should repeat these lines for about fifteen minutes, but if you are short on time, being alone for a few minutes will do the trick as well. When you are ready to start, repeat these affirmations:

- I NOW release all of my resistance to the flow of abundance, well-being, and wealth

- I WILL now receive the flow of well-being, abundance, and wealth into my life.

- I feel GRATEFUL for this flow of abundance, wealth, and well-being.

These along with the other great positive energies that you send out to the world will make a big difference in the amount of wealth and abundance that are attracted to you. It is a good idea to consider doing this a few times a day, perhaps in the morning and at night, to make sure that you are sending out these good energies as often as possible. As you can see, the process of affirmations does not have to be difficult, and you are going to love the results you get just by changing your energy and sending out the positive vibes, like those above, for a few minutes each day.

Chapter 6: Reprogramming for Healthy Relationships

Everyone wants to have healthy relationships. They want to have friends they can go hang out with when they are feeling down or need to have a night out. They want to have a good relationship with their family members, both their parents and their kids, to carry on traditions and have a sense of belonging. They want to have a good relationship, or find a good relationship, with someone who can be their soulmate.

While all of these relationships are important, the modern world has made it hard to maintain or even find these relationships. We are often busy trying to get things done, always at work, or trying to make ends meet. There sometimes aren't enough hours in the day to get these tasks done and maintain these healthy relationships, especially when everyone else is so busy. Plus, finding good friends with your best interests at heart or finding a soulmate can seem intimidating and almost impossible.

It is important to have these relationships, and if you are struggling in one or more areas of your personal relationships, there are steps that you can take with the help of affirmations to help you finally get and maintain these relationships for your health.

The first thing that you will need to do in this case is to set your goals. Is there an issue that you are facing when it comes to a current situation? Are you and your husband always fighting? Are you hoping to make some new friends because you just moved to a new area? Are you hoping to finally find someone you can share your time with because you are tired of all the other people you have given a chance to and who have failed?

You can have any goal that you want, but make sure that it is a positive one and that it is something that you want. You will not send out the right energies if you are just doing this because you think you need a partner since you have reached a certain age rather than doing it because you want it. Think of something that you would like to change when it comes to your relationships, no matter what kind of relationship you would like to work on, and then use this as the basis of your affirmations.

A good example of this is when you and a spouse may be fighting. Perhaps you have done some counseling or worked together and found out that you aren't paying enough attention to each other or aren't communicating properly. A good affirmation that you can use is something like, "I pay attention to my spouse to understand their feelings." It takes some work to reprogram the brain to start doing this, but using this kind of affirmation will make the subconscious more accepting to changing its behavior.

When coming up with an affirmation, you need to keep it positive. You may think that you are doing a good thing by using a statement like, "I don't blame my spouse every time that something goes wrong," but you have some negative words inside that could still make you angry and will send out the wrong kinds of energy to the universe. Negative energy is so bad to have around you. In fact, the use of negativity in your life, such as complaining about a problem in your relationship, can make it more likely that the issues will escalate.

For the example above, instead of using these hurtful words and bringing back more of that negative energy, it is best to say something like, "I always try to find solutions to any issues that arise." This is a much more positive way to look at things, and you will conclude that it adds more positive energy to your life.

The idea of innocent perception

Too many times we are already in a relationship and little things about the other person will start to annoy us. We may not like the way that they chew their food or how they don't help out around the house as much as we think they should. The adverse thing about this is that we are dwelling on the negative in our relationship rather than focusing on some of the good that we used to enjoy. We are adding more trouble to that relationship. We are forming our perception of the other person, and the longer we hold onto these negative thoughts, the worse the relationship will become.

One unique idea that you can encounter when you are working in a relationship is the concept of innocent perception. The best way to think about this is to compare the differences between a relationship with a partner that is brand new and that relationship a few months or longer down the road.

When you first get into a new relationship with someone, you look at them with rose-colored glasses. You may see some faults with them, but you are so enamored by the new relationship and excited to see where it goes that can accept some of these flaws and just ignore the rest. This part of the relationship works well. You are both sending out a lot of positive energy to the universe, and there is no fighting, just a lot of fun.

But over time, things begin to change. You spend more time together, or perhaps even move in together. You start to notice some of the flaws of the other person more, and they start annoying you. These flaws are the same ones that were there at the beginning of the relationship, but for some reason, they are more important, and you both begin to fight more over them. The more you struggle or feel upset that these flaws are irritating you, the more negative energy is going out, and eventually, you will probably break up.

Now, were those flaws that big of a deal? Yes, they were a bit of an annoyance, but were they worth the fighting? Was the other partner that bad? Most likely they were just little things, but you started to put some negative energy into the world about them, and it came back and ruined the relationship.

The idea of innocent perception is that you keep looking at your partner like you did at the beginning of the relationship. This does not mean that you ignore the flaws (everyone has them, and they will sometimes annoy you), but instead that you see them without placing guilt on the other partner. You see that by placing guilt and being annoyed all the time, you are just causing harm to the relationship. Sure, you can both talk about the little habits that annoy you about each other, but these annoyances should not take over the whole relationship. In fact, you should embrace these as part of the person you love as part of the relationship, to bring in that good energy and to maintain the relationship.

Innocent perception is not about ignoring what is going on, but realizing that these annoyances and bad habits are just a part of the relationship. Every relationship will have them, and if you love the other person, you will find that the innocent perception can help you focus on the best parts of the relationship rather than the bad parts.

Affirmations you can try

Ignoring the bad habits that your partner has, or the other bad things that you deal with during your friendships, can be tough. We want everything always to be perfect for us. But this is just not reality, and focusing on this can ruin many good relationships.

If you are looking for a way to improve your relationships, whether it is with a spouse or with friends, here are some affirmations that you can try out that will make a big difference:

- I allow those that I once saw as objectors to now be my supporters
- Everyone that I meet has a message for me
- As I change the way that I perceive relationships, my life feels more whole.

- I readily engage my energy to give to others, in agreement with what I want to receive from them.
- I think according to what I want from a relationship.
- I use innocent perception with all I meet.
- I no longer need the drama from others in my life. I feel at peace and am determined to dwell in reality.
- I inspire everyone I encounter.
- I honor and respect the choices of others.
- I approach new encounters with high expectations and openness.
- When I see someone, I greet them with as much gladness as possible.
- I surround myself with those who completely support me.
- When I use innocent perception, the actions of other will not threaten me.
- I have a genuine interest in other people I meet.

Exercises

There are many things that you can do with your affirmations as well as in your daily life that will help to improve your relationships. First, you need to learn how to focus on the good parts of the relationship. Yes, there are going to be things that annoy you, but for now, ignore those and just focus on the things in the relationship that make you happy. Is there something about the other person that makes you happy? What do you love to do with that other person? Spend a week focusing just on these good things, and ignoring the little things that may bother you, and you will be amazed at the changes that you see.

Next, remember to compliment the other person in the relationship. This is especially important when they may be doing something that is bothering you. For example, if your wife is nagging you or your husband is being lazy, take the time to appreciate all they do for you and give them a compliment for all the hard work. This may be a nice little change from the routine and can not only make them feel good but will bring more positive energy to the relationship.

If you are someone who is interested in writing things down, the next step is for you. A good way to affirm your relationships is to sit down and write out the ideal relationship. What would you most like to happen in the relationship to make it better? Write down anything that you want at first, but later, you will need to reframe these so that they become a positive affirmation.

Later, you will be able to use these writings as part of your relationship affirmations. For example, if you want a relationship that is fun and loving, you may consider saying an affirmation like this: "Thank you for my loving, caring, exciting, and empowering relationship." This helps to show that you are grateful for the things that you have and helps you just to concentrate on the good that is already there, while still telling the universe, or those particles, that you are looking for some more positivity in return.

Often the biggest issue with our relationships is how we perceive them. We go into a new relationship excited and with the ability to ignore the negatives or the things that may bother us. But something happens over time, and those little negatives start to take over the whole relationship. But when you learn how to use innocent perception to focus on the things that you are happy about in the relationship, and you start to use affirmations to bring about the best side of the relationship, and you are going to be so amazed at how great that relationship turns out.

Chapter 7: Better Time Management Using Reprogramming

Time management is a thing that most of us lack. We waste a lot of time in the day looking online, looking for things that we misplaced, checking emails, and so much else. This often leads us to fall behind in other aspects of our lives such as spending time with friends and family because we have to work late and into the weekend to just stay on top of our business.

Time management can make all of this different. It is a more efficient way to get the work done. It allows you to stay focused for as long as you need to do the job, to organize so that all of your items are in one place all of the time, and to avoid unnecessary time with others that will slow down your progress. There are many things that you can do when you are ready to add some good time management to your life, but you need to be willing to work on them. If you can do this, you will be amazed at how quickly you can get work done no matter how much you need to work on.

There are a ton of tips and tricks that you can following order to work on your time management. We are going to focus on how affirmations and your personal energy will be able to work together to help you properly take care of your time to ensure that you are getting everything done without all the stress.

Adding time management into your life

If you are like the majority of Americans who feel that they are always running around just to keep up and failing miserably in the process, it is time to add in a bit of management to get things done. Most people stress out so much about their lack of free time because they feel sorry for all the things they are missing out on when they try to get caught up on work. Over time, this stress is going to make you fall further behind and can even cause issues to your health all because of the negative energies that you are dealing with.

Affirmations are a great way to reduce some of that stress you are feelings so that you can focus on your work to get things done. This is going to help with your positive energy in two ways. First, it will contribute to reducing stress because stress sends out large amounts of negative energy to the universe. If you can reduce your stress, you can work on the positive energy. Second, if you can get your work done on time and get some free time to spend with your family and friends, you are going to feel relaxed and have fun, which can send out tons of that great positive energy.

Some of the affirmations that you can try out that will help to send out the right positive energy about time management include:

"When I keep on task, my work gets done faster!"
"Time management allows me to enjoy life, not just work all the time."

These affirmations help you to understand that time management is critical in all aspects of your life, whether you are doing work, trying to clean the house, working on school stuff, or getting something else done during the day. Everyone is busy, no matter what they do for a living, even those who stay at home with the kids, and it is good to use these kinds of affirmations to help get the work done with the support of positive energy.

Learning how to prioritize

Sometimes the issue that comes up with time management is that you aren't able to prioritize. You may spend an hour looking Facebook and catching up with friends or choose to look at lots of junk email right away in the morning. You may even work on a project that won't take much time, or isn't due for a few weeks, rather than working on that big one that is expected in a week.
All of us are guilty of it. We spend time working on something that is small or could wait until later, and then we are surprised when we are out of time and have to scramble to get things done. This adds more stress and more negative energy to the world, and you could end up with some issues in the process as well.

Learning how to prioritize can make things easier. It will ensure that you will get everything done on time without wasting time and without all the stress. Some of the ways that you can prioritize your life so that you get these things done and keep the positive energy up include:

- Do the important tasks first—this can be the big jobs or the ones that are due first but concentrate on them right away. It is tempting to work on those smaller projects, but if you waste so much time on them, you are going to cut into the time that is needed for the bigger projects and could add on more stress.
- Avoid social media— if you have work that needs to be done, it is best to stay off of social media. This is a big time waster, and unless you are working specifically on the Facebook page for your company, it is a waste of time.
- Save emails for later—a lot of people will get to work and start checking their emails right away. This may seem like a great solution, but most of those emails probably don't need an answer right away, if at all. Why not sit down and do some work first and get to the emails later on when you are caught up and have some free time?

- Get organized—organization is your best friend when trying to prioritize. It will hold information that you need so that you don't waste time trying to find the things that you need. You can even organize things so that you can jump right from one project to another, with everything you need present, without having to stop.

Less waste

If you are wasting your time, you are not doing well with time management. If you want to be more productive with the time that you have, you need to learn how to avoid anything that will waste your time so that you can spend it on working instead.

The first thing that you can do is to get rid of, or at least reduce, the things that will directly waste your time. This means you should turn off the phone, close the emails, and avoid going on social media. If you go down to the break room every hour and end up spending twenty minutes talking to people, you need to reduce how often you leave the office. Close your door so no one else can bother you if you need to get something done.

The trick here is to combine all the parts together to reduce the time that you are wasting and to ensure that you can maintain those good relationships and other parts of your life to keep good energy coming out you. If you are struggling with time management, it is time to bring in some affirmations that can make it all better. Some good affirmations that you can try include:

- I will cherish every moment.
- I know that my time is very precious and I refuse to waste any of it.
- I will make my time count.
- Procrastination is just of waste of time. My life is important, and I won't waste any of it.

What a lot of people don't realize is that they have plenty of time in the day. They have time to get the work done, spend time with family and friends, and even to relax. But when they spend so much of their time doing wasteful activities, it is almost impossible to keep up. If you work hard to utilize your time, you will find that the hours are perfect to get things done.

Exercises

Now that you know why time management is so important, let's take some time to look at a simple activity that will help you to bring time management into your life.

In this activity, we are going to do a visualization technique that allows you to find the time for your personal ideal day. You can pick whatever you want to happen on your perfect day, but this is going to help you visualize the goal so that it can become a reality for you. To get started, here are the steps:

- For about a month, make sure to add fifteen minutes to your schedule each day. You should pick out a time where you won't be interrupted for at least the fifteen minutes. If you are busy or have to deal with small children, splitting this into three segments of five minutes is fine.
- Now sit back and relax during the first of the five minute segments. Spend this time imagining what your ideal day would be like. Envision what it is like to wake up, get ready for work, and

move around. What are you doing throughout the day? How do you feel? Let your imagination go wild here and imagine the taste of things, the smells, the touch, and more. Remember that this is your ideal day, so all the images you have should be those that bring you pleasure.

- For the second segment, go back through this ideal day and just pick the portions where you are alone. The other images aren't unimportant, but if other people are there, it is hard to dictate what will happen in a situation, so for now we just need the ones where you are alone. Focus on these images and what you can do to make them even better, to bring about more pleasure in your day.
- Out of the pictures that you selected for the last step, identify a piece that you are able to actually duplicate today. Perhaps it is time that you took a shower. Or your drive to work. Or getting a few minutes to work out, read a book, or do something else you enjoy. It is best to pick out something that you really enjoy, but you don't often set time apart to do.

- Now take that one segment and add it into your day. Find some time that works best for you and just do it. You will be amazed at how much fun this can be and how relaxed it will make you if you just set a small portion of time apart to do the activity you like.

There are a number of benefits that you will receive when you do this exercise each day. First, you are going to work on your visualization skills, which can help to reduce stress, promote healing, and enhance your creativity, and who doesn't want those things in their life? You are also taking time out of your day to clarify what your values are and what you would like to be doing with your life. The more that you do this, the easier it will be to learn what will fulfil you when you make a decision. By doing this for fifteen minutes each day for a month, which really isn't that much time, you are starting a pattern that will be with you for a long time to come.

The best benefit of this is that you are proving that you have power. When you visualize that something good is going to happen in your day and then you set that time apart in order to accomplish the work, you are taking control and gaining the power. Nothing is better for your life and your positive energy than providing yourself with some simple pleasures each day. And when you learn how to be in the moment, a skill that you will learn with visualization, you are going to be able to focus on the good that is going on now rather than the bad that may have bothered you earlier.

Yes, at first this is going to seem a bit silly. You may wonder if daydreaming is going to do that much for you with just a few minutes each day. But visualization is not daydreaming; it is actively focusing on the things that you want and then going out there and getting them. It may seem a little strange at first, but after a week or so, you will get the hang of the idea, and it won't take long for you to see the results.

Chapter 8: See Your Stress and Anxiety Go Away

Anxiety is an issue that affects many people. To those that don't suffer from it, it may seem like a cop-out, something that another person will say to get out of a party or to avoid being social. But for those who are suffering from anxiety, it is an issue that plagues them all of the time. Those with severe anxiety will change their lifestyles to avoid going out in public or preventing certain circumstances so that the anxiety does not creep up on them.

This is not the way to live life. You are so much more than that and deserve to live a life that is free of fear and anxiety. This is not to put down those who are dealing with anxiety, but rather a way to let you know that you are valuable and are worth living the life that you want!

Getting rid of anxiety is important for several reasons. First, when you are dealing with anxiety, you are sending out a lot of negative energy that will just be returned right back to you. Every time that you go through an anxiety attack, you are attracting more of that energy, and it is more likely that it will affect you again. You are also avoiding social situations and anything that might trigger that next attack. This can make you live in fear, and you may always dwell on the things you are missing and on the fear, which just leads to more issues.

Luckily, using affirmations can help to limit the effect that anxiety has on your life and can make it easier to control your energy. Whether you just have anxiety attacks on occasion or you are someone who has changed their whole life around to avoid these attacks, these affirmations are going to help to center you and get things back on track.

Picking an affirmation for your anxiety

When it comes to feeling anxiety all the time, you need to pick an affirmation right away. You don't need to have the best one necessarily, but you need to pick one that resonates with you and start right away. You have already sent over so much negative energy from your anxiety attacks that waiting around will just make it all worse. Pick one and start an affirmation session right now before reading further. Here is a good one to start with:

"I release the control that anxiety and panic had over me. In this moment, I am safe. I am happy that I am living my life and that I can radiate out happiness and confidence to others."

Spend at least a few minutes saying this affirmation. Remember to add in the feelings and conviction, and you will already begin to feel better. After this, you will need to get into the habit of saying this affirmation each day. A good place to start is to write down the statement twenty times each day. Doing ten times in the morning and ten times at night is best so that you are reminding your self-conscious that you are wonderful and that anxiety is no longer the master of your life.

Over time, you are going to get so used to this that the affirmation will repeat automatically in your head. This can be helpful throughout the day if the anxiety starts to come back or you get a bit anxious. Just repeat your affirmation whenever you need some help and you will be able to take back control of your life without the anxiety.

This is a process that may take some time. Most people who have been working with anxiety have dealt with this issue for a long time. But that does not mean that you should give up hope. Simply find an affirmation that you can work with, stick it into each day and refuse to forget or skip a day. Believe in the good energy that you are sending out, and it won't take long before you start to notice a change in the way you behave and react to the things that go on around you. Anxiety does not have to take control of your life as long as you realize your worth and take control.

Chapter 9: Tips to Bring About Positive Energy

We have spent some time talking about how the different energies you send off are going to have an effect on the type of life that you have. When you send off negative energy by focusing on all the bad that is going on in your life, you are just going to get more of the same. On the other hand, if you can reprogram the brain and convince it to think about positive things to reverse the energy that you are sending out, you would be amazed at all the great things that can come into your life. The choice is yours. You can have the healthy relationships, wealth, success, and good health as long as you understand and learn how to change your energy.

Here are a few things that you can do to change the negative energy that you are sending out to something positive to improve your life!

- Set boundaries—sometimes you just need to set boundaries to live the life that you want. For example, if you waste an hour or more on emails a day, you are cutting out some of the time that you could spend doing something else. You could set a boundary by just checking emails one time a day for twenty minutes. Now you have an extra forty minutes a day that you can use as your own rather than wasting it online. You can do this with many other things such as setting limits on work, setting limits on how much time you waste at meetings, and much more.

- The thing about the positives—yes, there are times in your life when negative things are going to happen. But why waste all your energy focusing on the bad? You are fantastic and worth so much in life. Why not focus all your energy towards this and see what amazing results you can get? You are the one who gets to control what energy you are sending out, so focus on the good and get so much more back in return.
- Use your affirmations—we spent a lot of time talking about affirmations in this book and how they can be used to help reprogram your mind. We are trained to focus on the wrong and feel horrible because things are not going our way. But this is not the right way to see success or the

right way to get the things that you want. You need to learn how to reprogram your mind to think about the things that you want in life and to focus on the positive if you want to get out of this rut and start living the life that you want.

- Visualize what you want—visualization is one of the best ways that you can send out the right energy. Sometimes words just don't do the trick, but when you imagine what you want and then go out there and get it done, you are convincing your mind that you are in control and that anything is possible.

- Be consistent—you are not going to get the results out of this if you aren't consistent. There are so many people who will get excited about affirmations and quantum physics that they will try it out for a week or so and then they give up. They may forget a few times or assume they just don't have the time. These are the same people who state that affirmations don't work because they didn't see the results that they wanted. If you want to send out the positive energy to the universe, your affirmations and positive thoughts need to stay consistent. You need to have fifteen minutes set aside each day so that you can focus on retraining your mind and getting it to behave so that you send out those positive energies all the time. You just won't get this by missing the time you set aside, only doing it for a short amount of time, or messing around.

- Realize that you are the one in control—the most important thing that you can do is to remember that you are the one in control. If you believe that negative things are just a part of your life and that the universe dislikes you, you are going to be right. But this is not because of anything the universe does wrong; it is because of the negative energy that you are sending out. When you start to realize that you are the one who gets to control your destiny, you will work harder to keep those thoughts positive so that you can live the life you deserve.

Positive energy can do so much good for your whole life. It can bring you the wealth, happiness, good health, great relationships, and everything else that you want in life. You just need to understand how your energy is affecting the other particles around you to see that when you send out the positive energy, you will be able to get so much more of it back to you!

Conclusion

Thank for making it through to the end of *Quantum Physics to Get What You Want: Practical Quantum Physics Tips to Improve Your Life, Attract Health, Happiness, & Money*. Let's hope it was informative and able to provide you with all of the tools you need to achieve your goals, whatever they may be.

The next step is to get started with making the changes that you want in your life. You have the destiny to bring health, wealth, and happiness to your life. No one else is in charge of this, and you have no one else to blame if things aren't going the way that you want. You only need to make some changes in your energy releases and learn how to turn your emotions into powerful tools that work for you.

This guidebook is going to give you the tools that you need to use quantum physics to see success in life. While most people will dismiss quantum physics because they think it has nothing to do with their lives, it is incredible how much it can control the outcome of your life if you let it. Take control and work on getting everything that you want!

I wish you all the best on your journey,

Maya

www.ingramcontent.com/pod-product-compliance
Lightning Source LLC
Chambersburg PA
CBHW071411080526
44587CB00017B/3241